LONDON ABC

ILLUSTRATED BY
BEN HAWKES

DOUBLEDAY

LONDON

A   B   C

A   DOUBLEDAY   BOOK

978   0   857   53187   2

Published in Great Britain by Doubleday, an
imprint of Random House Children's Books A Random
House Group Company This edition published 2012

1   3   5   7   9   10   8   6   4   2

Copyright © Random House Children's Books, 2012 All rights
reserved. No part of this publication may be reproduced,
stored in a retrieval system, or transmitted in any form or by
any means, electronic, mechanical, photocopying, recording
or otherwise, without the prior permission of the publishers.
RANDOM   HOUSE   CHILDREN'S   BOOKS
61–63   Uxbridge   Road,   London   W5   5SA
w w w . k i d s a t r a n d o m h o u s e . c o . u k
w w w . r a n d o m h o u s e . c o . u k
Addresses   for   companies   within   The   Random
House Group Limited can be found at: www.
r a n d o m h o u s e . c o . u k / o f f i c e s . h t m
THE   RANDOM   HOUSE   GROUP
Limited   Reg.   No.   954009
A CIP catalogue record for this
book is available from
the   British
L i b r a r y .
P r i n t e d
and   bound
in   China

WELCOME TO LONDON!

London is one of the most famous and iconic capital cities in the world. It is busy, bustling and full of treasures for you to discover. It's a centre for fashion, films and food, business, the arts and entertainment. Plus it's filled with countless museums, galleries, theatres, sporting grounds, shops, markets, parks and palaces. We are excited to show you some of these in this ABC!

Most of all London is full of stories – its history stretches back over 2,000 years, and it has been immortalised in hundreds of books, TV series and movies: from Dickens's Victorian London, to the London of Sherlock Holmes, Mary Poppins and Doctor Who.

We can't wait for YOU to explore London and start your own story. There are so many ways to discover the city: on foot, finding hidden side streets; on the underground (do you know which colour is for which line?); on red London buses or in black cabs. Remember to take care crossing the road and always have an adult with you!

And don't forget to take this book with you too. On each page there are lots of things for you to spot beginning with that letter. Some are London things and some aren't! See if you can spot them all, and then turn to the back of the book to check your answers. We've also suggested some other London landmarks for you to seek out. And see if you can spot what our lost little penguin friend is up to as well.

Have fun exploring the London in this book, and the real-life one outside your door . . .

A IS FOR **AQUARIUM**

EXIT

B IS FOR  **BIG BEN**

E IS FOR
EYE

F IS FOR FISH & CHIPS

H IS FOR

FREE HUGS

HYDE PARK

I IS FOR

I ♥ LONDON

chocolate VANILLA STRAWBERRY

J IS FOR JUBILEE!

K IS FOR **KEW**

L IS FOR
LORD
MAYOR'S SHOW

MUSEUM

M IS FOR **M**ARATHON

MAP OF LONDON

21

156

N IS FOR NELSON'S COLUMN

HAVE YOU SEEN THIS PENGUIN?
P
IS FOR
PICCADILLY
CIRCUS
Luigis

Q IS FOR QUEEN

QUIET PLEASE

chocolate VANILLA STRAWBERRY

T IS FOR

TOWER BRIDGE

U IS FOR O UNDERGROUND

CHAPMAN 2

MACDONALD 2

W IS FOR

WIMBLEDON

Y IS FOR

YOGA

YIPPEE!!!

Z IS FOR **Zoo!**

DID YOU SPOT?

A IS ALSO FOR: Anchor, apple, aquanaut

B IS ALSO FOR: Bearskin, bicycle, black cab, boat, bobby, bridge, Buckingham Palace, bus

C IS ALSO FOR: Camera, case, cat burglar, crown, cushion

D IS ALSO FOR: Dog, door, doorknob

E IS ALSO FOR: Elephant, English flag (St George)

F IS ALSO FOR: Fedora, fire bucket, fire engine, fire hose, firemen, fish, football

G IS ALSO FOR: Gallery, gentleman, Gherkin, glasses

H IS ALSO FOR: Hair, hat, hedge, helicopter, helmet, horse, hot dog, hugs

I IS ALSO FOR: Ice cream, ice-cream van, insect, iris, iron gates

J IS ALSO FOR: Jelly, jug, juggler, juggling balls

K IS ALSO FOR: Kate, King (to be), kiss, kite, kitten, knitter

L IS ALSO FOR: Ladder, lamp post

M IS ALSO FOR: Map, monkey, monocle, monster, moustache, museum

N IS ALSO FOR: National Gallery, necklace, newspaper, newsstand

O IS ALSO FOR: Octopus, onion, ostrich

P IS ALSO FOR: Pear, penguin, people, phone box, pigeon, pizza restaurant, post box, poster

Q IS ALSO FOR: Queue, quiche, "quiet please" sign, quilt

R IS ALSO FOR: Rain, reading glasses, red wine, roast beef, roast potatoes, rose, royals

S IS ALSO FOR: Sailor, screen, sky, sportsmen, sprinters, stands, sun

T IS ALSO FOR: Taxi, Thames, tiger, Tower of London, traffic, tugboat

U IS ALSO FOR: Ukulele, umbrella, uniforms, Union Jack

V IS ALSO FOR: Van, video camera

W IS ALSO FOR: Wasp, wellies, whites, worm

X IS ALSO FOR: X marks the spot, x-ray, xylophone

Y IS ALSO FOR: Yawn, yellow, yoga, yoghurt, yo-yo

Z IS ALSO FOR: Zebra, zookeeper

LONDON LANDMARKS FEATURED IN THIS BOOK

Big Ben
The British Museum
Buckingham Palace
Downing Street
The Gherkin
The Houses of Parliament

Hyde Park
Kew Gardens
King's Cross Station
Leicester Square
The London Aquarium
The London Eye

London Zoo
The National Gallery
Nelson's Column
The Olympic Park
Oxford Circus
Piccadilly Circus

Regent's Park
St Paul's Cathedral
The Serpentine
Shakespeare's Globe
The Statue of Eros
The Thames

Tower Bridge
The Tower of London
Trafalgar Square
Westminster Bridge
Wimbledon

OTHER LANDMARKS FOR YOU TO VISIT

The Albert Memorial
Apsley House
The Bank of England
The Barbican
Battersea Power Station
The British Library
Broadcasting House
Carnaby Street
Charing Cross
City Hall
Cleopatra's Needle
Covent Garden
Cutty Sark
Fortnum & Mason
Foyles

Green Park
Hamleys
Hampstead Heath
Hampton Court
Harrods
HMS Belfast
Highgate Cemetery
Horse Guards Parade
Imperial War Museum
Kensington Palace
Liberty
Little Venice
Lloyd's of London
The London Dungeon
The London Transport

Museum
Lord's Cricket Ground
Madame Tussauds
The Mall
Mansion House
Marble Arch
The Millennium Bridge
The Monument
The Museum of London
The National Maritime
Museum
The National Portrait
Gallery
The National Theatre
The Natural History

Museum
The O2
The Old Bailey
The Oxo Tower
Paddington Station
Peter Pan in Kensington
Gardens
Portobello Market
The Ritz Hotel
The Royal Albert Hall
The Royal Observatory
The Royal Opera House
The Science Museum
Selfridges
Smithfield Market

Spitalfields Market
South Bank
The Southbank Centre
Southwark Cathedral
Speaker's Corner
St James's Palace
St James's Park
Tate Britain
Tate Modern
Theatreland
Twickenham
The V & A
Wembley Stadium
Westminster Abbey